Instant Confidence:

92 Tips On How To Build Confidence To Develop Self- Confidence And Self- Esteem

By Gary Vurnum

www.92Tips.com and
www.Vurnum.com

Instant Confidence: 92 Tips On How To
Build Confidence To Develop
Self- Confidence And Self- Esteem
ISBN: 1451519176
EAN- 13: 9781451519174

For Katie, Skye, and Connor

"Never change who you are for someone else. There will always be enough people who will love you just for being you."

"Want To Give Your Self-Confidence A Massive Boost? The FREE 9 Critical Steps To Immediate Self-Confidence Special Report Will Show You How..."

FREE

In this Special Report you will discover...

- Why removing one single word from your life will have an *immediate* positive impact!

- The one-second change to your thinking that will *forever change* how you look at yourself!

- Why changing your focus away from you will help you become more confident.

- How just a few minutes now and again can have a *massive* impact on how you feel about yourself.

- PLUS a special gift worth up to $120!

Go to www.SelfConfidenceFormula.com/free

Even the most successful people have limiting beliefs about certain aspects of themselves.

1

The ONLY difference between you and them is that they instead choose to focus on their strengths instead of their 'weaknesses'!

Make a commitment NOW to start acting more confidently, even if you feel the opposite!

2

'Fake it til you make it' does work in this case – and you would be surprised if you knew how many famous people in the public eye do exactly that – appear confident even when they don't necessarily feel it!

Look people in the eye when you talk to them, or stand up straighter than you normally do.

3

Don't worry about trying to walk confidently into a room and being the center of attention – just work on acting and speaking just a little more confidently than usual.

Make the decision that you don't say anything about yourself that you wouldn't want to come true.

4

The more you practice talking about yourself in a positive manner, the more you will unconsciously start believing what you are saying — whether it is true now or not!

You should NEVER compare yourself to other people.

5

For a start, you'll always find something to mark yourself down against them with, and secondly, many of those people who appear outwardly confident actually are using their bravado to disguise the fact that inwardly they actually have very little self- confidence!

Self- confidence is not all about the impression you give other people.

6

More crucially, it's about how you truly feel about who you are, where you are, and where you want your life to be.

Try and think about the positive things in your life as you lie there just before you go to sleep.

7

You won't believe the influence that doing this one simple thing can have, not only on your night's sleep, but also on how you feel when you wake up!

Try and get yourself to smile a few times every day – even if it is only to yourself!

8

Everybody has a least someone, something, or a memory that makes them smile - so even if you don't feel particularly happy about where you currently are – SMILE!

You can't change your past, but you can change your future!

9

Sure – your upbringing has influenced who you are now, but take it from me, confidence (or lack of it) is not a hereditary thing! If this was the case, then by now there would be generation after generation of the same families becoming more and more confident (and successful) with other families becoming less confident!

Positive thinking alone won't suddenly make you a more confident person.

10

But...I can guarantee you that there are NO confident people on this planet who don't think positive thoughts about themselves, what they feel they can achieve, and how they view where their life currently is!

Promise yourself from now on that you will only sow positive 'seeds'.

11

Look for the best in situations wherever you can, and, when things go wrong, look for the silver lining rather than the cloud. Take it from me based on my own experiences – there is ALWAYS something positive you can take out of any situation, even if it is only a reminder that certain things in your life are more important than others.

Both 'good' and 'bad' things shape us as a person.

12

However, as we're conditioned to place more importance on the negative things in life, we forget that we DO have some good things happen to us too!

Remember that you don't have to be loud to be self-confident.

13

There are many more people than you can imagine that are 'quietly confident' who don't feel the need to go around telling the World how great they are! You'd also be surprised to discover that most loud people LACK self-confidence, and are just using a 'front' to try and cover it up!

You must commit to doing whatever it takes to be more a more confident person!

14

Remember – if you continue to do the same things in your life you're going to get the same result!

Make a sincere attempt to do small things that made you nervous.

15

Yes, I know that this is a big step (even if, in the grand scheme of your life, it is really a tiny little step) – but unless you start challenging yourself then things are always going to be the way they always have been, aren't they?

It's time that you accept full responsibility for your life.

16

You must take responsibility for the setting of your goals, the path that you take towards them, as well as for taking any other steps with your life that must be taken – no matter how uncomfortable they may be!

You need to assume that you are responsible for everything that has, and will, happen in your life.

17

You can't get your mind in the right position for taking charge of your life going forward if you refuse to take charge of where you are now, and what it has taken to get you there!

How would it make you feel to be more responsible for EVERY area of your life?

18

It can be hard to become more accountable for the things you do – but just making an effort to do so will give a fantastic boost to your self-esteem and confidence as, believe me, you are capable of so much more than you could ever dream possible!

Remember – focus on small, achievable things first.

19

Then, once you get into the habit of taking on more responsibility, it will be so much easier to aim for the more 'bigger picture' stuff! Deep down, you KNOW what you should or shouldn't be doing – and NOW is the time to finally start moving towards taking charge of your own life!

Everyone has problems that they are ashamed of, or wishes were different.

20

Self-confident people choose to face their problems head–on, as they know that they stand more chance of putting things right if they are proactive instead of reactive to the situation.

Resolve to face up to your problems rather than ignoring them.

21

Ignoring the negative things in your life may help in the short- term, but it seriously messes up your life in the longer term!

From now on accept full responsibility for ALL of your feelings.

22

YOU are the sole person who is in charge of their emotions – nobody else! You're not going to suddenly turn into a positive thinking machine overnight so, of course, you're still going to have negative feelings about yourself and what you're capable of.

Your self-confidence depends on you accepting responsibility for who you are, and where you are.

23

It's time that YOU took on the role of the sole person who is responsible for everything in your life – 'good' and 'bad'.

Whether you like it or not, it will take a little time to build up your confidence.

24

After all – it's taken a lifetime of conditioning to get you to where your current confidence levels are, remember!

You will have to take risks!

25

Yes...there will be times when you begin to question whether all the effort is really worth it! This is why it is critical that you find a way to keep yourself motivated to keep yourself moving forward – even when things aren't going to plan.

Basically, you are either motivated by a fear of loss, or by the chance of a reward.

26

Everything else you may read about motivation revolves around this single element – so it's important that you know how you 'operate' – either by fear or reward! Once you understand this - then you need to have something to aim for! You need to have goals that really inspire you that you have a very good reason for wanting to accomplish them.

You must have something in your life that inspires you with a passion!

27

It must be something that he achievement of which gets you out of bed in the morning! Once you have that – then it is so much easier to stay motivated, no matter what happens.

Don't take comfort in the attention that other people give you.

28

We've all met people who feed off of others who complain all day long about how bad their life is — but YOU must make sure that you are looking to achieve more out of your life, rather than dwelling on what you're not currently happy with!

Your self-image is the lens through which you see yourself.

29

More importantly, it is how you believe OTHER people see you. The sad thing is that, for the vast majority of people, this self-image is completely WRONG in the sense that they believe that other people see them and their abilities more negatively than is actually the case!

Make a commitment to make an attempt to work towards your goals whenever possible.

30

You will never lose by going after something that is new and challenging – as, even if you appear to fail – you are still growing more as a person, and moving one step closer to finding out the best path for you to achieve your goals.

Imagine with feeling what it is like to achieve each of your goals.

31

Try to visualize with as much detail as possible, as the more 'reality' you can put into your visualizations (such as touch, taste, smell, and feelings, as well as what you see) — the more chance of your brain interpreting them as if they WERE real — which is the whole point of visualization.

Think of something you can do to take the first step to making your main goal into a reality.

32

Just do one thing. Anything! It doesn't matter how small it is — whether it is just doing some research online, or making a phone call. Just start!

Self-confident people very rarely procrastinate.

33

This is because they act first, then worry about the next step AFTER they act! Too many people get bogged down in the details, or feel that they need to know every single step towards their goal before taking action – and all they end up doing is...nothing much at all!

Commit to reading self-help books EVERY single day, without fail.

34

If you prefer to listen to audios, do that instead. Just find something positive and uplifting. The more you 'feed' your mind with positive, life-affirming words and images – the easier you will find it to see the positives in your life, and the easier it will be to think more clearly about what you really want from it!

Without some form of determination – you're not going to get very far in your life.

35

If you've lacked self-confidence for a long time, then, without some serious determination on your part, things aren't going to change very much – nor very quickly!

You CAN change ANY part of your life, not just your self- confidence.

36

You just need the determination to stick with it long enough to start seeing results. And...once you begin feeling more self- confident, you'll find it so much easier to push forward than you can believe possible.

Let's face it — if you didn't really want to change — you wouldn't be reading this would you?

37

Yet — as it's so much easier to just stay in the comfortable pattern of your current life, then just pushing your comfort even a little can be a major 'decision'. It's time for you to make that decision!

You will definitely need to pay some form of 'price' in order to change.

38

It may come in the form of time, effort, stress or uncertainty. Focus on the fact that you are actually going to get a huge long-term benefit from a more confident you. You'll often be surprised to discover that a lot of the things that you may believe may 'hurt' to get rid of actually become quite easy to replace!

You need to engage your emotions in this entire process of wanting to change.

39

Your feelings (good and bad) about who you are and who you want to be are critical to making lasting change.

Write a summary of the benefits that a more confident you would have on your current life.

40

Put them on a small card. Keep it with you where you can look at it regularly. If you feel it will help, then print it out in big letters and put those benefits on your wall.

How you think is extremely important in regards to being more self- confident.

41

Whether you believe in the more spiritual side of life or not, there is certainly no denying that you can change the quality of your life by changing how you think about it.

Every single action you take is preceded by a thought.

42

Therefore, doesn't it make sense for you to focus on lining up your thoughts in a positive, solution- oriented manner BEFORE you actually do anything?

Try to think like a confident person, and you will automatically feel more confident!

43

Remember – the ONLY thing you have 100% complete control over are your thoughts. This means that it is entirely down to YOU whether you CHOOSE to consciously select thoughts that support a positive, new confident you, or ones that just reinforce a more timid, more negative and less confident you!

Start consciously becoming aware of whether what you are thinking about.

44

Consider whether these thoughts actually help you become more confident or not. You need to help 'train your brain' to focus on the positive and empowering instead of the negative and disempowering!

Get into the habit of changing how you speak when you are thinking about doing something.

45

Remember – for most of us, our automatic response is to tend to look for the negative (i.e. about obstacles, and what we "can't" do), so talking more positively may seem a little challenging at first – which is to be expected!

If you're not going to look out for yourself and your well-being, then nobody else is!

46

You need to start appreciating that you ARE a worthy person, and that you ARE somebody who deserves all that they want from life!

How you come across to other people is a reflection of how you think about yourself.

47

This means that it's time that you stopped 'beating yourself up' and started to appreciate yourself more!

People aren't magically born self-confident.

48

They learn how to be from the people close to them. What this means is that you don't either have a confidence 'gene' or not – ANYBODY can be self-confident and grab life by the horns and really live it!

By saying yes more often – you will begin to open yourself up to more that life has to offer.

49

Take it from me, you'll soon see that there are many, many things that you are ALREADY incredibly accomplished at without you even realizing it!

It's easy to let your negative thoughts spiral out of control.

50

This downward spiral will sap your confidence, and will always make things seem a lot worse than they actually are. Of course, if you've always been the sort of person who tends to focus on the negative, then it's no easy task to convert yourself to a more positive thinker!

A thought can only come about if it is linked in some way to the thought that comes before it.

51

This is why it is so easy to get your thoughts into a downward spiral, as each negative thought builds upon the last. So – it's essential that you make the effort to catch yourself thinking before your negative, disempowering thoughts run away with themselves.

Affirmations are powerful (if used properly) – as they also involve you speaking.

52

Adding your voice to affirm your thoughts brings them 'out into the open' – and by doing so, you automatically add a new level of power and energy to what you are thinking about.

Success in anything is never a 'one-shot deal'!

53

You need to keep practicing being aware of what you are currently thinking. So...set your watch to beep every hour – and stop just for a few seconds, and catch what thoughts are flying around in your head. What are they telling you about the quality of your thoughts? Are they generally productive, positive thoughts, or are they more focused on the negative?

Nobody is born with a negative voice in their head!

54

The style of that voice is a product of your upbringing and has been influenced by the people and events so far in your life. The good thing about this is that, if you have created a voice with a negative slant – this means that you can ALSO undo it – and nurture an inner voice that is more positive and supportive!

Spend some time today trying to listen in to what that voice in your head is talking about.

55

Remember – what it is saying is only a reflection of what your CURRENT beliefs about yourself are – they aren't set in stone! So...what are you thinking about and how does it reflect on who you are?

When a negative thought appears, just say to yourself "Stop"!

56

Even better – if you're able to say it out loud, then your voice will add more power and conviction to the process. Once you catch the thought – ask yourself why you have thought that way. Even though the thought is negative, or not very helpful – it STILL appeared for a reason.

Your subconscious offers thoughts up because it is reflecting your own opinion of yourself.

57

Therefore, not only is it good to catch the thought itself – it is also extremely valuable to spend a little time considering WHY it appeared in the first place!

*No matter how hard you try —
you cannot NOT think!*

58

Not only that, it's also impossible to think two thoughts at the same time. (If you don't believe me — try and see if you can do it!) This is why it is so critical that you don't allow your negative thoughts to build up one upon another.

It's no good just catching yourself thinking negatively and then not doing anything about it!

59

You need to get into the habit of REPLACING your negative thoughts with more positive and empowering ones.

Get into the habit of looking for a more positive 'spin' on everything.

60

Look at each negative thought you have about yourself and what you are capable of. If some thoughts are so negative that you can't easily find a more positive slant on them – instead just replace them with more generic or less specific positive thoughts.

If you're struggling, focus on something or someone who makes you feel warm inside.

61

I use an image I have in my head of my daughters smiling and laughing. Now try thinking negatively. I guarantee that, if you ARE really smiling for real — then you won't be able to!

How you imagine yourself to be is not based on what is possible.

62

It's based on your beliefs and experiences of what you believe you are capable of, and we both know how limited (and incorrect) they can be! So — you need to start using your imagination to support what you are trying to achieve, rather than to hold you back!

You're always focusing and sifting everything in the world around you, based upon your beliefs.

63

So – the more you can work on your self- belief, then the more your subconscious will automatically 'find' more of what you are looking for – and bring it into your life.

Your imagination isn't something that you should have left behind in Kindergarten!

64

It is a very powerful tool that, if used properly, WILL change your life. So – just go and have some fun with it!

The key to using your imagination effectively is to use as many senses as you can.

65

Most of us only tend to imagine through sight alone, but the more you can bring taste, touch, smell, and noise into the process – the more quickly you will achieve the results you want.

Visualization isn't a tool just for 'new age' people who meditate!

66

You are actually doing it ALL of the time without even realizing it — usually to negative effect! For example...how many times have you imagined that a particular situation isn't going to work out — only for it to literally turn out exactly as you expected it? This is why it's so important that you start using it in the correct way!

It's critical that you get into the feelings of how confident people behave.

67

It's important that you understand that how you feel about what you want to achieve is more important than what it actually is!

Don't worry about spending hours (or even minutes) visualizing what you want.

68

Just get in, feel great about what you're visualizing, and get out as soon as it isn't inspiring any more. That's the secret to really making visualization work!

You must pretend to be the person you want to be first!

69

If you don't, then your chances of becoming that person in reality become much slimmer! For example, when you speak and act more confidently – even if you are really only pretending – then you will automatically feel more confident. The people around you will immediately assume that you are confident, and will treat you accordingly!

If you act timidly, other people will assume that you are like that and treat you accordingly.

70

This then reinforces the very personality traits you're trying to change! Of course you will feel uncomfortable when you try to speak and act as if you were more confident. Your mind isn't used to this new way of acting, so it will struggle to adapt to accepting the 'new you'. However, just like when you learn to ride a bicycle – if you persevere, then you cannot help but get there.

Many of the most self-confident people are actually plagued with self-doubt inside.

71

Outside they may give the impression that nothing fazes them and that they are in complete control — yet they may well be having to deal with the exact same doubts as you are!

Success leaves clues — and where learning from confident people is concerned — this is no exception!

72

The term 'modelling' is used to describe how you can learn from the people whom you wish to aspire to be like. It's based on the fact that you can avoid unnecessary problems and challenges if you find someone who is already where you want to be, and learn from them!

Find something that you really like, or are good at — and aim to be an expert in that.

73

When you are doing something well — the confidence will just flow out of you, without you even realizing it, and other people around you cannot help but react to that.

Success at anything is dependent on you taking it step-by-step.

74

How do you climb up a ladder? One step at a time. How do you build your self-confidence? One step at a time. Reading about becoming more confident is one thing, but the only way to truly learn something is by doing it!

It is certainly worth the effort to make a regular attempt at taking on things that challenge you.

75

This is because the more times you push your comfort zone – the easier you will find it to do so again and again...and again!

Everyone feels fear – even those people who appear amazingly confident!

76

You just need to force yourself to ignore that fear, take a big gulp, and take action despite of it! Most of the time, you'll actually be surprised to discover that what you experience is absolutely nowhere near as 'bad' as the fear made you imagine it to be!

Don't try to make huge changes overnight, or push yourself too far too quickly.

77

Moving forward is all about how your subconscious views the risk of changing against the possibility of the reward for doing so. Their subconscious just 'snaps back' and forces them to get back to where it feels 'safe' – which then manifests itself as your motivation grinding to a halt, or you feel that that continued effort isn't going to be worthwhile. Sound familiar?

You need to do something practical about improving on your self-confidence every single day!

78

This way you are taking small risks by changing in small ways – which therefore gives your subconscious less reason to rebel against you. Whenever possible, try to mentally rehearse and visualize what you are attempting before you do it for real.

Why people fail to achieve much is more down to a lack of preparation than lack of action!

79

I am not for a moment suggesting that you need to know absolutely everything about the goal you are aiming for. All I am saying is that you need to gather as much information and knowledge as you can so that you can be prepared for the times when things may not go according to plan.

The best thing to do is ALWAYS to take action first then deal with the outcome of that action.

80

Do not spend a lot of time over-analyzing possible outcomes, or possible pitfalls as you will never get anything done – ever!

Everything in your life is a result of what has gone before.

81

So, what this means in regards to your confidence is that it is the result of how you responded to those who raised you, as well as the environment in which you grew up.

Remember – when you were born, you didn't automatically lack confidence!

82

This came much later, once you began to interact with the world and the people around you. Your confidence (or more accurately, your lack of it) was learned, most of it in your early childhood. It developed when you really didn't have much say in who you were or what you did, so it's a useful exercise to try to understand what happened in your past that set the tone for your adult life.

Even the most happy and self-confident people make mistakes, and have huge failures!

83

The only difference is how you might react to your failures compared to them. There is a great saying that many positive people use to look at how they view their failures. They call it 'Failing falling forwards' – which basically means that, as long as you learn from your 'failures', it means that you're just one step closer to success!

Depending on where you are and who you are with, your confidence levels can vary hugely.

84

Ever thought about it in that way before? For example, there are people who are very dynamic and successful at work who consistently have bad relationships, and many geniuses who can't speak to others outside of their work environments.

When you look at yourself in the mirror, what sort of person do you see in front of you?

85

Is it someone you are proud of or someone who you wish could be happier and do more with their life? You MUST be proud of who you are — even if that person isn't currently the one you see. I bet that over the years you HAVE had times where you have felt great about yourself and the direction of your life. Tap into those feelings whenever you feel as if things aren't quite going your way.

Much of what shaped your confidence happened before you were consciously aware of it.

86

This is why it's a worthwhile exercise to take a look back (however painful) to see what you can learn now that you have a better understanding of how to become more confident.

Above everything else, it's how YOU feel about YOU that is the most important thing!

87

You must be your own 'greatest fan', otherwise you will struggle to maintain your confidence if things ever don't quite go in the direction you want them.

Make a point of doing one thing every single day that you enojoyed as a child.

88

It doesn't matter how silly it is, or how stupid you look...just do something which releases that Inner Child to live life to the full! Make the effort to look for the funny side of every situation – just as a young child would. Yes – you may feel a little ridiculous at first, but believe me, the feelings of sheer enjoyment you will get will soon stop you worrying about how you may look!

Take up a hobby that requires you to use your imagination.

89

Whether it is painting, making music, writing creatively, crafting, or even acting and dancing, it doesn't matter! Apart from making you just enjoy life more, the very act of creativity, imagination, and visualization will help you in ALL areas of your life by allowing you to see that there is so much more you can do with it than just acting 'all grown up' like you feel that you should!

We all make mistakes, and have many things that we wish we had handled differently.

90

You wouldn't be human if you didn't – so stop beating yourself up about it! It's time that you learned from your experiences and allowed yourself to move on. What's important is who and where you are NOW! Leave the past where it belongs – in the past!

You don't have to be the 'life and soul of the party' in order to become more confident.

91

Just do it step by step – YOUR way, and focus on building up your confidence in the areas of your life where you already feel more comfortable about who you are.

Now, just get on and do it!

92

Yes, it will be uncomfortable –
but remind yourself that, as the
great Napoleon Hill once said
'Whatever the mind of man can
conceive and believe, it will
achieve'. The more you focus on
seeing and feeling yourself being
a more confident person, the
greater chance of your success!

"Want To Give Your Self-Confidence A Massive Boost? The FREE 9 Critical Steps To Immediate Self-Confidence Special Report Will Show You How…"

In this Special Report you will discover…

- Why removing one single word from your life will have an *immediate* positive impact!

- The one-second change to your thinking that will *forever change* how you look at yourself!

- Why changing your focus away from you will help you become more confident.

- How just a few minutes now and again can have a *massive* impact on how you feel about yourself.

- PLUS a special gift worth up to $120!

Go to www.SelfConfidenceFormula.com/free

Discover more "92 Tips" and "92 Affirmations" at www.92Tips.com

"Nothing is ever as hard, or as complicated, as you think it might be. Just give it a go and you'll see!"

10402777R0

Made in the USA
Lexington, KY
20 July 2011